Living on the Difference

Acknowledgements

Versions of some of these poems have appeared in the following publications:
Brando's Hat, Essex Competition Anthology 2003, Equinox, Lancaster Litfest Competition Anthology 2002, Magma, The North, Poetry Nottingham International, Other Poetry, Penniless Press, Pitch, Smiths Knoll, Staple, Thumbscrew, Trewithen Chapbooks 2 & 3, Ware Competition Anthology 2003.

'Winter Coat' won First Prize in the Amnesty International Competition 2002.

Living on the Difference

Mike Barlow

Smith/Doorstop Books

Published 2004 by
Smith/Doorstop Books
The Poetry Business
The Studio
Byram Arcade
Westgate
Huddersfield HD1 1ND

Copyright © Mike Barlow 2004
All Rights Reserved

ISBN 1-902382-63-3
Mike Barlow hereby asserts his moral right to be identified as the author of this book.

British Library Cataloguing-in-Publication Data. A catalogue record for this book is available from the British Library.

Typeset at The Poetry Business
Printed by Charlesworths, Huddersfield
Cover picture: 'Broken Moon', construction by Mike Barlow
Author's photograph by Jane Routh

Distributed by Central Books Ltd., 99 Wallis Road, London E9 5LN

The Poetry Business gratefully acknowledges the help of Arts Council England and Kirklees Cultural Services.

CONTENTS

7	Winter Coat
8	Meeting The Man In The Street
9	The Special Correspondent Goes To War
10	Double Booked
11	If You Were A Spy
12	The Absent House
13	Dark Matter
14	Out After Dark
15	Treading Water
16	The Cellar
17	This Isn't About Me
18	Orbiting
19	Interference
20	Initiation
21	Idle Talk
22	Skeleton Key
23	Pendulum
24	6 O'clock Tuesday
25	The Day's Bite
26	Teak
27	Nuisance Calls
28	Interlude
29	The Silence
30	Shadow Eater
32	The Difference

33	Brief
34	The Pathologist Finds a Lover
35	Forensic Angel
36	They
37	Believe This
38	Gate Fever
39	Getting The Time In
40	Trespasser
41	Gamekeeper's Son
42	No Trouble Between Us
43	Heirloom
44	Microsurgery
45	Chosen Tree
46	On The Eve
47	Sortie
48	History
49	Peat Wraith
50	A Sabbath Vigil
51	Island Watching
52	Lip-reading at Port an Droighionn
53	The Special Correspondent Waits
54	Rolling
55	Offshore with Edward Hopper

Winter Coat

We were dancing when they came
but the four four of heavy boots put paid to that.

The chill sent us indoors to dig out what we could
for warmth. I found my uncle's greatcoat from the war,

heavy, drab and mildewed, but double-breasted,
with brass buttons and a collar I could hide behind.

It taught me how to stoop, to shuffle and queue
like an old man suffering from damp and memory.

I patched the lining with bits of coloured rag,
embroidered words there, whatever came to me:

tomorrow, sweetheart, polka, apricot, yesterday,
and the names of friends I'd never see again.

Sometimes I'd stand out on the corner, whip it open
like a flasher, then run for the shelter of an alley.

One night I dreamt thunder, woke to hear the city sigh,
as if a heaviness had just passed down the street.

Dead leaves scratched the pavement.
Across the yard someone tuned a fiddle.

Today we're in the square again, dancing.
I wear the old coat inside out, sweat a fever underneath.

Meeting The Man In The Street

Our first encounter was in a transport caff
on the Great North Road. He was a thin man
with a pudding-basin belly propped
against the counter. Through his open shirt
the blue wing of a tattoo flapped. It wasn't the way
he slopped tea over the bacon sandwiches
or dropped ash on the eccles cakes. It was how
he closed his eyes when he gave you change.

Some years later I was jostled on the Tube
by a fat guy, all body odour and shiny suit.
I wouldn't have given him a second thought
except that he looked at me to apologise
and my whole life flashed by.
I got off at the next station and walked.

These days we meet more often.
I'll be picking my nose in a traffic queue
then find him watching from the next car.
Or we'll end up face to face in a crowded street,
he'll dodge left, I'll dodge right, mirror images,
trying not to look at one another.

Today I've come to the canal to daydream.
Conditions are just right. A slow rain stipples the water.
My rod's set up. I watch the float, hoping
it won't move much. The bloke ten yards along
gets up to stretch. He walks this way, offers me
a sandwich. I can tell he wants to talk.
If you could see into my brain, his eyes declare,
your hair would stand on end.

The Special Correspondent Goes To War

News has always found me, the way static
on a mountain top stands hair on end.
I have this curse for place and time.

The gas explosion on the way to school,
the beach closed by oilspill, the war criminal
suddenly exposed, his picture window bungalow
two streets from my maiden aunt.

At first they'd send me anywhere –
chance stabs at a map – knowing how
my chemistry would bond with race riots,
ethnic cleansing, paedophiles.

Now I'm doorstepped, dogged by paparazzi
with their bikes and cameras. But this way
any news I might attract belongs to them.
So I have to slip out in disguise.

A month ago in full drag I left a young hack
with his eyes watering. Last night I carried
a Kalashnikov right past them. Events shrunk back,
sloped off down alleys like second thoughts.

Two days ago I took an axe
to the editor's Mondeo. No one's reported that.
Tonight I'm looking through old cuttings,
searching for a pattern I can jinx.

A can of petrol comes to mind,
some charred remains (not mine),
a fresh start – a war zone no one's heard of yet.

Double Booked

Four storeys up and our attic room double booked.
All evening we worried we'd get back to find our bags
pitched on the landing, a stranger sprawled on the bed.
But here's a place mistakes correct themselves
as the breathless young Swede bounds two at a time
up a hundred steps to tell us no one else has shown.

Headlines next day had me thinking sniffer dogs
and figures in paper jump suits scouring the room
for skin flakes. The photofit the papers carried
looked familiar. The Virgin Guard? The taxi driver?
The white van's registration only a digit away
from the blue Polo we sold your brother.

And can you account for your movements
this time last month, a week ago last Wednesday,
the day before yesterday even? What's more to the point
can you account for mine? Next time we take a break
we'll double book and lay a false trail.

If You Were A Spy

You'd quote me Wordsworth as I pass:
*Dust as we are, the immortal spirit grows
Like harmony in music;*
your face uncrackable as code
awaiting my reply: *There is a dark
Inscrutable workmanship that reconciles
Discordant elements...*

Nor would you bat an eyelid
as dangerous ideas pumped round my heart.
You'd sacrifice your flesh to mine.
You'd do it for your country, let me in
without a visa, steal my DNA.

In the middle of the night
you'd slip out like a dream,
phone in to your anonymous controller,
download my fantasies
from a chip secreted in your navel.

If you were a spy I'd not see you again,
except as a distant figure in a crowd
who might be someone else.

The Absent House

Nights now the current of sleep cuts out,
jerks me conscious. I disentangle from our leglock,
slide from the bed's raft, push through dark to find
beyond the bedroom door the house is gone:
a maze of shadows and a slight stir in the air as if
the words that chose us yesterday won't let things rest.

Across the valley's black lake hills rise up,
car lights sweep round a bend, crest a hump then sink.
Caught there in a stranger's skin I cast a prayer up
to the crush of stars, step forward like an astronaut
towards a world caught at its end or its beginning.

Behind me both our threads unravel,
yours in sleep, mine finding its own way out.

Dark Matter

2 a.m. There's a bright new sun
low down in the east where I'd expect
Jupiter to transit Gemini –
Cowkins' halogen yardlight
triggered by a stray leaf
or a cat after mice.

If I could make dark matter
I'd dump a load right now,
fork it over their gate, scatter it
round the yard, spread it on meadows
to leach into land drains, the run-off
washing downriver to swallow light waves
the whole length of the valley,
extinguish floodlit mansions,
obliterate street lights, cut car beams
with the abruptness of a head-on crash.

I'd post some to the City Council.
As the young clerk slit the envelope
the illuminations round Morecambe Bay
would pop their bulbs, permanently fused.
We could look up then and find our way
from Cassiopeia to Aldebaran
with all the time in the Universe
to contemplate Andromeda
hurtling towards the Milky Way
at three hundred thousand miles an hour.

Out After Dark

My friend Dave and I once spent a whole day
fishing by the backwater where a month before
the farmer had shot himself. There was this pool
where you couldn't fail but nobody went there now.

We took a sliced white loaf and lit a fire to cook on.
But we caught nothing and ended up
rolling the bread into putty grey balls
and toasting them on sticks instead.

As dusk crept up on us we fed the fire
and let the heat plate our hands and faces
while the night leant its cold plank
against our backs and made us shiver.

He told me then how once his Dad
got so drunk they found him next morning
unconscious and half naked on the front path
and had to call an ambulance.

And I told him about my uncle
who was mad and lived in an asylum
and who, when he visited talked all day
to the invisible people who gave him orders.

We pissed on the fire and watched the last embers
winking in the steam then set off home
through a thick moonless dark where the shapes
of trees were giant bulls breathing down our necks.

For being out late and panicking the family
I went straight to bed. I lay there with the light out,
shivering as I looked up at the ceiling
and imagined the night sky full of fish.

Treading Water

I learnt the art of treading water early,
clinging to his shoulders
as he swam the river from the garden end;
he'd give the word and I'd let go, the pause
before he turned and caught me
lengthening each time.

Later we'd cross side by side
to the far bank, stand on the bottom,
feet slithering on roots and rocks;
from this fresh angle gaze back at the house
to see it as a stranger might;
exchange a few words, what was meant
still left in the air unsaid.

In mud-brown rivers now
I celebrate this buoyancy,
strike out for the middle where
the land's a place apart,
the memory of his voice
amplified across the surface,
carrying an awkwardness as if unsure
exactly how to put things.

The Cellar

The bare bulb my father hit his head on
stuck down from the ceiling at an angle,
its crooked pool of light tilting at empty boxes,
the broken pram, an armchair with its stuffing out,
a spade with a snapped worm-eaten shaft.

Cold shadows watched me, breathed dust.
I'd catch their voices in the scuff of mice,
the crack of plastic in a draught.
And if I thought out loud to reassure myself
I'd feel a footstep cross my grave.

Once the river flooded, three feet of water
unlocked it all. From the top step I'd look down
on empty paint tins, broken planks, a scuttle
bobbing in a scum of dust, hear a splash
as something swam across the dark.

At night my father would return from work,
strip to underpants, descend by torchlight, wade
waist deep to fill the meter with tomorrow's shillings.
Watching him I'd think of Venezuela where, I'd read,
piranhas could reduce a man to bone in seconds.

This Isn't About Me

I was a forty a day man but then this isn't about me.
It's about you and how much I'd forgotten:
your swathe of black hair, hands and face
grimy from days on the road, nights in the cab,
egg and chip breakfasts, steak and mash lunch,
one fag after another lit from the previous dimp.

I'd forgotten that look in your eyes
like a dirty joke you didn't know whether to tell.
I'd forgotten your wife's complaints
about video recorders in the wardrobe,
the conviction for 'doing battle',
the big grin when you got off with a fine.

All I'd remembered were the balloons of your cheeks
deflated and hung from boughs of bone,
strands of grey hair across a blotched scalp.
If you'd been your father you'd have looked like this.

You lay still in starched sheets
among flowers you'd never see at home
where your five kids fought you for every inch.

We tried the usual banter but the jokes fell flat,
the clank of trays, squeal of castors on the rubber floor
enough to ruin anybody's punchline.

When I left I threw my last full pack in the bin.
It took a week or two for my wife to tell me
I tasted different when I kissed her.

Orbiting

I lie in the bath
watching a piece of blue sky
the shape of Australia drift eastwards.

I'm an astronaut returning home
contemplating time and gravity,
the perils of re-entry.

Yesterday my daughter phoned, in tears.
She doesn't watch the News,
do drugs or guilt.

She'll swim a mile before work,
get drunk at weddings,
argue the toss with a Jehovah's Witness.

But a friend just back from Bosnia
needs to talk. Now she's a child again,
wants answers nobody can give.

Twelve billion years away
a beam of light has knocked
our theories of the Universe for six.

It absorbs the wrong photons,
wobbles fundamental constants
and even bends the truth.

Back in orbit
it's time to pull the plug,
brace myself for turbulence.

Interference

Your voice crackles with distance.
You're only a mile away
across town but the line picks up
a seawash, the whine of a wind
carrying every fourth word
to another continent.

From the window here I watch
street lamps snaking on the water
as the last boat working from The Quay
slides upriver, turns, its lights
revolving red round green,
to head down on the tide.

A year ago you phoned from Oregon,
your voice so clear I felt you next to me.
I heard the sea then as you described
the drum of big Pacific rollers,
a high tide's slap against the pier.
Now I can't catch what you say.

I'm drifting with that small boat where,
in an hour's time, two figures
will be paying out their nets
on the tricky waters of the bay;
Fleetwood will be visible, a faint
scar of light separating sky from sea.

Initiation

Tradition cradles you.
They do things properly here,
family gown, silver spoon,
godparents awkward
in their best suit and new outfit.

The font is Cotswold stone,
the fingered water a fleeting sign
of something everlasting,
the roar above, a bomber taking off:
six hours to Baghdad.

I'm the figure hovering
beyond himself, the great uncle
you'll not hear much about.
I bring good will
and something else.

Besides your mother's calm,
your father's grounding in the land,
I wish you the gene
for restlessness, for change,
for being counted.

In everybody's line
you'll find a suffragette
or a lone sailor,
that particular face
challenging the camera.

I watch your stare.
It takes in what it can. Some things
make sense already, others not,
just random noise
and dark shapes in the sky.

Idle Talk

That's all it was – floods and forecasts.
Rain erased the edges of the town,
the swollen river curdled where it swept the quay.
Without a change of tone you said:
*My wife's taken our three-year old to live
two hundred miles away with someone else.*

I watched the bow-wave round the bridge,
a builder's plank as it rafted to the sea.
I didn't know you well enough
for an arm around your shoulders,
couldn't trust myself
with anything you'd want to hear.

Once I'd faced what you were facing. Nothing
anyone told me then made any difference.
So I stood beside you, out of touch
and lost for words, unable to account
for how you get from there to here.
Beneath us both the water creased and eddied.

Skeleton Key

It's midsummer. The calendar still shows February's snow.
I've no idea what day it is. The village shop and the supermarket
open all day Sunday now. I'd read but my mind slides
over words as if they're meant for someone else. I try music.
Bach doesn't do it for me, nor does Jerry Lee Lewis.
The telephone rings. Wrong number.

I move up behind you as you peer out of the window.
Geese graze the meadow in B-movie rain.
I imagine a figure in a trilby and trench coat
trying doors and windows. His gloved hand slips
down an inside pocket for a skeleton key. I tell myself
this is an old black and white one. It'll be alright in the end.

I run my finger down your spine. You give me what
my father would have called an old-fashioned look.
I don't know what it means but it seems right
for the occasion: a day the key won't fit the lock
between yesterday and tomorrow, a day we'll unpick
with a bottle of wine, discussing the meaning of life.

Pendulum

Serious discussion you say?
Like when it's half past midnight
and I push the slabs of sleep aside
to sit bolt upright in my head.
Or it's the end of a long journey,
we switch the engine off and listen
to it cooling under the bonnet.
Last time you stole my best lines.
Remember? All I could do was nod.

You pick at a frayed cuff and speak
with a hand half covering your mouth.
The signs aren't good; inside us
ideas neither dares admit to; behind us
there's a door ajar – and silence:
the hall clock must have stopped.

At times like this I find it best
to keep to practicalities, feel the chain
between my thumb and finger, winch
the weights back, lift the pendulum
just far enough to one side
to meet its arc, sense the fine
inevitability as small cogs mesh. Listen:
the tick we count on without knowing it
resumes, moves on.

6 O'clock Tuesday

Think about us. Now. A mutable event,
you drinking whisky, me picking at a dish of peanuts
while we plan the vegetable garden,
new geese and a summer wedding party.

Nothing controversial. We drift into the evening,
content. I'd say we had it licked. And yet
already I'm unsure of what I've said, what sense
you'll give my words tomorrow, what part I'll give you.

That sharp glance thrown my way
you may not be aware of.
What you pick up from me I've no idea.
We take our chances.

The Day's Bite

You lie in bed watching midges at the window
while the colour of the evening ripens.

Asleep in the bath, I dream of the ways
the day has bitten us: the sweet roast smell

of mown hay, pollen clouds
lifting from the valley, watery eyes,

a thistle-splintered hand, your caught breath
when the hammer slipped,

the oncologist's letter hurriedly stuck
behind the milk jug on the dresser,

a hare frozen in stubble, ears flat
against the soft brown boulder of itself,

the root of earlies too small yet for supper,
a black toad squatting in the rushes.

Teak

A five foot stack of teak planks
shifted from the barn floor to the loft.

I should have been deterred by dust and splinters
but midwinter froze my reasoning
and a sudden dread of atrophy
got the better of the surgeon's words.

So I set about in the stone cold air,
wrenched, lifted,
found a point of balance
and with elephantine grace

carried each plank like a tightrope walker's bar
through the obstacle course of tractor,
mower, cluttered bench to lean
end-on against the cross-beam.

A year or two. Don't rush.
Take a holiday. Somewhere exotic.

No more than six I told myself, then rest.
From the ladder top I hauled,
levered, shoved. With a clap and clatter
each plank landed on the loft deck.

Under slates and purlins
I stooped, knelt, crawled
setting the new stack straight,
stickered and square.

Six then rest I'd said, but carried on,
sweat squeezed like juice,
heady with the breath of work,
the peppery dust of Burma at my throat.

Nuisance Calls

At first it was a singing wire through my brain,
the electricity of thought I thought.
Then birdsong, the occasional chaffinch,
blackbirds, a thrush, a whole dawn chorus,
often in the middle of a winter afternoon,
sometimes so loud
I'd have to turn up Beethoven to escape.

In the end though it was starlings who took over,
mimicked lawn mowers, rushing water,
the creak of a stranger on the stair,
the front door bell, curlews.
Finally they got the telephone off pat.
They ring at all hours now,
even interrupt my dreams to reach me.

I'd answer if I could,
just to hear myself above the din,
what's being said behind my saying it.
I imagine heavy breathing or a white noise
like a woodpecker drilling its way out
through my skull.

I'd answer and say nothing,
straining for the hint of silence,
the click of the receiver
at the other end.

Interlude

Whenever I go out I make sure music's playing, something
to leave its echo in the empty rooms I'll be returning to.

If I'm to be gone a while, I'll put on Bach's cello suites.
The pure sounds always last the longest.

If I'm just off shopping, the sun's out and the blood's up
I'll turn on Credence Clearwater and give my age away.

Once I forgot my filofax and interrupted Smetana in love,
the forests of Bohemia so fresh I felt a stranger in my own home.

One day I expect to come back to heavy metal axe marks
in the front door or find the curtains ripped by saxophones

or the brickwork crumbling where the whole structure
trembled at the knees while Leonora rescued Florestan.

The Silence

I've carried it inside me all my life,
somewhere between my abdomen and epiglottis.
It follows its own seasons, swells like ripe fruit
plugging the larynx, or shrinks to a stone hard pit.

When I was younger they feared me possessed,
spoke loudly, mouthing each syllable
as if I were deaf or simple. It flourished
in the blank stares I chose to answer with.

When I speak now it shivers like a conscience,
troubled by what I might not mean, cuts me off
mid-sentence, plays cat and mouse with words,
scrambles syntax. I go unheard in meetings.

From time to time it blossoms, insists on space.
I'll disconnect the doorbell, unplug the phone.
Printed words become a chanting mob
so all the books get shelved, newspapers binned.

Bass winds might tune up in the chimney
or rain make idle talk against the windows.
I sit, count breaths. The stove ticks. The alembic
of the gut ferments, the blood's hydraulics roar.

Eventually, in full flower, it'll have me to itself.
I'll listen out for currents in the air,
my thoughts retreating voices in a garden.

Shadow Eater

It leant towards me in the kitchen
as if offering itself,
the place where its mouth was
coming to meet mine inexorably.

But I managed a side-step
with a deft bite at the right ear.
It tasted of charcoal.
I was constipated all day.

The next morning I evened up,
took off the left ear. The nose followed,
the edges of uncombed hair,
the biscuit of skull.
Within a week I was lightheaded.

You tried to steer me, spoke my name,
pulled me by the hand,
but when I explained you let go.
Gravity bled from me.

I swallowed the legs to leave
the torso a headless blob,
a gingerbread man's body
on a plate of light.

When I'd finished I walked on air,
my heart a small bulb pressing
at the paper thin walls of my chest,
knees and ankles lurching
through each ungrounded step.

At night I'd gather my wits
in a corner of the ceiling,
peer down on the two of us and wonder
who it was you whispered to
as you stared into my eyes.

The Difference

This is what'll happen. The painter
painting the sky will drop his brush
so crumbs of soil stick to cerulean blue;
or the fiddle player chuck his bow
and begin a pizzicato with his teeth.
The white foxglove will revert before our eyes,
geese ungaggle and the old wood
uproot itself and move a mile upstream.

The milky way will unravel
as we skinnydip above the weir.
Or thunder will circle the valley all night;
I'll fall asleep counting the seconds
between lightning and thunderclap.
In the morning the air will be so clear
we'll have to whisper
so Doreen up the road can't pick us up.

The radio will retune itself whenever
we hear the pips, the doorbell ring
when the toast pops, the smoke detector
scream as you open the fridge, the lights
fuse when the garden tap's turned on.
You'll put my shirt in the freezer
and the cod steaks in the wardrobe drawer.
You've done it before, I know,
but this time will be different.

Brief

Listen. Outside are waves of traffic, sirens,
air-brakes and the clack of high heels.
A single voice in front of you could drown.

Do not assume anything.
The tide of clues you're sifting through
could be in flood or on the turn.

Nod your head to show you're listening.
A child's cry from the street may be a song
or vice versa.

Make eye contact. Conversations
can confuse, mimic radios
tuned to different stations.

Say as little as possible.
Words feed on themselves.
Fictions multiply among them.

Avoid twiddling thumbs, twirling pens.
Ignore the voice in the other room
talking to the ansaphone.

Do not expect to meet someone you recognise.
Do not interrupt. Even the scrape of a chair
may break something.

The Pathologist Finds a Lover

Consider this body, abandoned,
crew overboard, last meal
half-digested, navigator
circuit on, dreams beyond reason.

Here there's only chemistry and limbs,
a sprawl obeying laws
of muscle, cartilage and tendon,
the subtle hints of history on skin;

one ankle's crooked, the right arm rakes
across the bed, and dangling from a wrist
the hand about to drop, as if a cough
or slammed door's all it takes.

The torso's statuesque and the mute drone
of sleep accompanies the caged beast's
rise and fall. There's a surgical scar,
with promises of screwed and stapled bone.

Smaller details bear inspection too:
the shiny crust where the toenail's gone,
ingrown or crushed, still caught perhaps
in nightmare jaws that won't let go;

one eyebrow thinned by eczema,
creases loosened round a drooping mouth,
the chipped tooth from a fight or fall,
the rancid breath of a meat-eater.

Rapid eye movement disturbs shut lids,
confessions in a soundproof room. Lift one
you could be staring at the soul, a whirl
like anti-matter. Blink, and you're sucked right in.

Forensic Angel

You hold your hand up to a guilty plea.
It's noted. As are the skidmarks, scorched brakepads,
starburst of windscreen, alibi conceived
in panic, then thought better of. (The dabs
on the steering wheel would have clinched it anyway.)
You want the rest t-i-c'd, the kicked down door,
the threat to kill, the tears, the hurled ashtray,
the fact you'd had a drink or two before.

You'd bend my ear if you could. Save your breath.
I'm not for listening. I'm simply here
to watch the shape your shadow makes, to guess
the weight of your soul, guard it when you're angry,
massage it when you're weak. I must be sure
when you eat your words your spirit won't go hungry.

Note: *'t-i-c' is legal shorthand for offences 'taken into consideration'.*

They

said you only had to look into his eyes
to see a stranger; a doorstep child
they called him, who made no sense
however hard they tried.

They remembered his collections of things in jars,
old nails, bone bits, ring-pulls, the errands
for the widow his lame mum cleaned for
who wouldn't hear a bad word said against him.

They frowned and shook their heads
at the cat found in the dyke, the coping stone
chipped from the bridge and heaved onto the track,
the silly laugh, the dry stare if you showed him kindness.

Nor were they surprised when his name came up
although he'd long since left the parish
and the brick house on the marsh was derelict
where once his Dad bred pigeons
and his no good bloody brother came and went.

They knew a thing or two they said, not telling
when the police came to the door, for that
was years ago when their unkind stares
could never have anticipated this, his picture
on the News and everybody's knowing nods
beginning to make some sense of things at last.

Believe This

She said to meet her at her mate Donna's.
But she knows I can't go there.
Our Jason grassed Donna's old man up.
Got three years.

So I mooched down town,
hung around the pier, met this bird
I used to go to school with, Charlene,
all legs and arse.

We got chatting like, then ended up
back at her place. Her folks are out
and I'm just getting somewhere
when her brother rolls in.

Now I know this bloke.
Squared up to a screw when I got nicked.
Got extra days himself.
So I owe him.

He gives me the nod
then we all have a brew and a spliff.
Suddenly he gets up and goes
we're doing the Mini-Mart, coming?

I didn't have a clue about the gun.

Gate Fever

His cellmate couldn't wait,
banged up with a nutter who wrote
each night to the wife he'd strangled.
You can't sleep with your hand
half way to the buzzer.

He'd always argued his release date,
now a week away;
pleaded with the Governor,
mithered Welfare, gone sick,
tried to hang himself.

Thinking itself merciful the Law
had listened, heard provocation
in the dead girl's taunts,
the night shifts when he'd not know
if a stranger or a friend were in his bed.

Four years. A stir at the back.
Call that Justice? He agreed.
But mercy was cruel,
would yet remit a third of this

to bring him here, the sentence
he'd always dreaded looming:
gates open to a life
no walls could keep safe.

Getting The Time In

He's not right suited.
It's cold and there's folk about.
Came up to get his time in.
Six hours at six pounds an hour. Cash.
Beer money, a present for his granddaughter,
a day out for Madge.

Different days each week.
No routine. His business.
They'd like to know,
but they won't.

The plumber's van by the barn.
One to watch, that Mick,
even at school. Snitched
when they battered third years
for dinner money.
Soft too. Wouldn't fight.

So he pulls his hat down,
tries to walk without the limp.
Takes off with the chainsaw,
down to the woods, out of sight.
Stays there, stays at it.
Even when his back gives.

*Just you watch it lad. All it takes
is some nosy bugger to make a call.*
One day he'll slip, the saw snag
or his back take for good in the valley bottom.
Until then its different days each week.
His business. Cash. Getting his time in.

Trespasser

He'd always had a straying instinct,
a tendency to lose the beaten path,
find bog and moving scree
or wade knee deep in a tide of heather.

Stopping to read the feathers of a kill
or listen to the tinnitus of larksong,
he'd find himself alone
and far from where he'd set out for.

Catching a dog's bark on the wind,
the shout of men with guns,
he'd close his eyes, imagine taking off
with the whirr and clack of grouse,

come alive on the lift of air,
even though they had him in their sights.

Gamekeeper's Son

Main beam on. They squeaked it
from the wood edge, wary,
brush dragging, eyes gold
in the glare of lights. One shot.

Aye, his old man said,
*I wouldn't care to stand
at three hundred yards
and live on the difference.*

He brought the body up to show her.
A vixen. *Beautiful* she whispered
at the fine teeth, the delicate feet
she wanted to touch but didn't.

No Trouble Between Us

Without looking up we'd feel his broad stoop
cross the window, cap pulled down, torn coat
belted with twine; hear the ring of the gate or squeak
of a shippon door, a barked command,
the lame dog slunk back against the wall.

And somewhere his two sons
about their business, the one who grinned
and wore his cap like his father
loading bales onto the trailer, the other
who wouldn't meet your eye, off out of sight.

We'd all shaken hands once. Neighbours.
There'll be no trouble between us. But we'd see
the loose-box at the track end and feel fenced in,
or grow uneasy strolling by the beck, glance up
to catch the dip of his silhouette against the skyline.

When we'd meet it'd be *Now then* and a sentence
clipped to the bare bones of itself. Once we passed
the three of them walling the lane to the ford. The dogs
came snarling for us. He took his time to call them off,
grudged us a nod. *Aye. They don't like folk.*

Heirloom

It's a single barrel, bolt action four ten
with an axe mark on the stock where the old man
once had to fend off Mad Will, who used to work for us
when he was sober. We kept it in the same place,
under the big bed in an old wax coat,
the bolt and box of cartridges on the top shelf
of the kitchen cupboard, back left corner.

Last time I used it was the summer night
I heard the crump of dynamite down by the river.
As I reached the wood a moon jumped out
between the clouds and of the two figures I saw
one I could swear had a familiar limp.
I was shaking so much my finger snatched
and I fired at the sky. Then it was dark again.

I live alone out here, don't take to visitors,
apart from Mad Will's nephew. He limps up now and then,
leaves a dozen eggs for a bottle or two of homebrew.
I've noticed lately how he looks me over, a sly squint
trying to work out what I know. I'll tell him one day
all that shotgun's ever hit in three generations
is his uncle's axe blade and a poacher's moon.

Microsurgery

I was down at Three Mile Bottom, turning winter swedes.
It was a day as clear as vodka, the smoke of trees
rising to dark veins against a flawless sky, rooks circling
Jenner's Copse. A figure staggered down the track
to Danny Pearson's place. Something wasn't right
but what went on on his land was no concern of mine.
Ever since he'd come at me with mad bull's eyes
and a mole wrench swinging in his hand to start the game
of writs and enough solicitors' letters to paper a parlour,
I've kept my side of the fence down here on Bottom Brook.

Ten minutes later the chopper passed so low you could hear
the thwack of rotors on the air like a slack drive belt.
I made no connection then but every time I hear one now
I imagine the old bugger passing above me,
a drip in his good arm, his half-severed hand in a bucket of ice.

When he was back I went up to see him. He stood across the yard
deliberately looking the other way, while his old lady
peered through me from the kitchen window, weighing
every beat of my heart in her unforgiving scales.
As he turned I dropped my offered hand. He smiled,
the flare in his eyes like the last flash of sunset.

We gathered his spring barley in good time,
got a fair price, put new drains in the top meadow
and between us relaid the boundary fence.
Its snakes about a bit but it'll keep us straight for a while.

Chosen Tree

It's not the tallest,
the most muscular,
the most ancient,
nor is it the one whose branches
give most shelter, but it carries
the scars of being here most visibly.

A band of dates, initials,
runic scratches
carved as high as a tall lad's reach.
Cut vows, gouged troth, forevers,
territory marked with pocket knives
and sharp stones.

I rub my fingers
on bumps and ridges,
the weathering of interwoven lives,
find my own initials,
swollen now and closed in
where once I'd made a clean true cut.
And next to mine, yours
bringing a smile's sap to my lips.

I think of all the scars
staying here in one place has brought.

On The Eve

What I'll remember of today is yesterday,
how it started with an east wind chilling the sun
then dropping to catch us out with the scent of gorse.
I'll remember dozing by the sound of water, river smell,
dippers, the cobble beach digging fists in my back;
the knitted maze of toadspawn in the pond;
and from the woodpile the zigzag flight
of a yellow brimstone tracing puzzles in the air.

I'll remember dusk, a small church silhouetted on a hill.
Inside, the altar cross removed, sixteen souls
in candlelight. Vigil. Silence. Readings: the Koran, Basho.
Each flame a meaning – or not. An old woman nods asleep,
a child fidgets against her mother. Pews
harden with the hour. Outside there's a moon
so bright you can count sheep on the opposite fell.
The yew trees in the churchyard promise an enduring sleep.

I'll remember how my dream of running water
kept on turning, became an army on the brink,
two hundred and fifty thousand voices
making a last call home.

Sortie

High pressure expected to continue,
the footsie down, price of crude up.

In a clear sky someone's writing,
loops of contrail smudged white in the jetstream.

The pasture's so hard footsteps ring in your head.
Buckets are iced up, the gate-catch frosted stuck.

In town little changes. The lighter man
has an extra line in football scarves.
Someone's put MacDonald's windows in.

We buy the usual week's supplies,
arrive back to the day's first sortie,
roof-high thunder flattening the senses.

Hands to our ears we crouch, shopping scattered.
In the top meadow geese are panicking.
Before the next plane's on us we make the house.

They're homing on the chimney stack
you shout, going for the shotgun.

History

Past crumbling gun emplacements
and the corrugations of old lazybeds
the road ends at a slipway where a broken boat
folds its sides in like insect wings.

She takes his arm along the beach.
The sea removes their footprints.

Beyond them, gale-driven drizzle filters light.
There's a rainbow hidden in the air.
From an ungrazed island
meadowsweet and clover scent the wind.

He stumbles, grips her sleeve,
some memory breaking in his stride:

perhaps a headland where a child
peered into the salivating sea;
a view from a window to a stack of creels;
a tin roof drumming in the rain;

or a small dip where he hid,
counting the flashes from the skerry buoy
as voices from the house called him,
called his name.

Peat Wraith

At the estuary brown water bleeds
into a turquoise sea. The land behind
is drenched and glutted, quakes to your tread.

A troubled sky shadows a moor mined
with bogponds, their iridescent skins alive.
Cottongrass trembles in the wind.

Peat stooks and cutters' shacks divide
old diggings. On the hagged horizon
half-caught movements trick your eyes,

as if someone's up there, on their own
watching you watching, a weight
of silence tossing to and fro.

You can get caught out, driving late,
when a spectre in a Kirlian cloud of moths
jumps through a dead spot in your lights.

Black-buttered face, beard of cats-fur moss,
he's sniffing for that sweet smokesmell
you can't get rid of in your clothes.

Wind up the window or he'll suck your breath,
leave you hollow, a myrtle-scented wraith.

A Sabbath Vigil

Nothing on the road.
Wind in the wires.

Drawn curtains, closed doors,
the shiver of reeds and ragwort;
geese hang mid-air against the wind.

A procession of cars,
dark suits, best coats, set faces;
a heron stabs the shore.

The ferry closed,
one rogue boat on the tide;
uneasy sea spits over rocks.

Returning cars, engines
murmuring like prayer;
a blue rent opens in a lagging of cloud.

Nothing on the road.
Wind in the wires.

Island Watching

Last month there were two days when the Sgurr
broke through sea-hugging cloud like a submarine,
and one morning you could also make out
Rum's full set of sails heading west.
The rest was an endless drag of grey squalls,
the buckshot of rain against the window
and a wind that nearly had the roof off.

I built this house high, as somewhere to aspire to,
closer to the gods who rule this place
than most considered safe, but overlooked by no one.
Sheep and stoic cattle nudge my walls
and on a clear day if I'm lucky a whale
or pod of porpoises will show, their brief
dark flashes like a rough weft in the sea.

Since none of you have joined me yet I keep
a look-out on my own, long nights
leave the lights on, stare out through the window
at the ghost room mirrored there, imagine
you enter one by one with gifts of city tales,
while the skerry light winks steadily beyond
and the lost shapes of the islands beckon us.

Lip-reading at Port an Droighionn

The evening air's so clear the peaks of South Uist
sit on the horizon like separate islands,
demonstrating how the earth curves.

They change shape as we watch,
tops flatten, grow lumps and limbs,
slopes steepen into cliffs

then stretch blue tapering fingers
along the level slit of sky
they seem suspended over,

demonstrating the particular way
warm air at sea distorts the light,
substituting mirage for reality.

And as the gauze of darkness thickens
I lose your lips' quotation marks. You speak
and what I hear you haven't said,

demonstrating what can happen
when you navigate by vowels,
lose sight of consonants.

The Special Correspondent Waits

I lip-read gossip, chain drink tea,
watch the waitress in the mirror,
buy strangers meals for news
I can't make news of yet,
how Geordie's boat's been gone two days
and no one's shown a face
at the big house for a week.

From time to time
I phone my column inches back,
walk round the dock,
my thoughts like kites
tugging at some truth.

What started with a rumour –
a body on a beach – turned out to be
a sea-logged bale of hemp
snagged in a creek, a strip of police tape
twitching in the breeze.

The only thing you can be sure of next they say
is the spring tide, low pressure belting in.
Across the estuary plovers scud,
an old man trudges
from his beached boat, digs for worms.

He treads the shoulder of the fork,
levers, lifts, shakes, bends to fill the bucket,
treads the fork again.
I sense the way news
breaks down here
like a quick shift in the current
you only notice out at sea.

Rolling

His canoe's state-of-the-art, custom fitted:
grablines, throwlines, velcro loops, you name it.
White water's his element, drawn to stoppers and boils
like a caddis fly. A capsize brings a screw roll
so accomplished you'd think it was staged.

Only when he's beached, prising his body
from the cockpit do you notice
the shrivelled leg, the wetsuit loose and baggy,
then the shuffle, the half hop to keep his balance
and the rolling limp exaggerating sea-legs.

We stop for a pint, take a stroll by the river.
The muddy path eels its way as we follow
a dipper's bob and flit upstream. At the weir
we look into a silver crease, the broad mane of foam.
Get that wrong he says *you'll not know which way's up.*

Suddenly he's down, foot caught in a tree root.
A parachutist's roll this time, and a full glass of ale slipped
from one hand to the other with the timing of an acrobat.
Before I know it he's bounced upright again,
crooked legs and crooked smile, not a drop wasted.

Offshore with Edward Hopper

There's a stiff breeze at our backs. We're tacking
north west on a steady swell, keeled over
with a fast sea washing the leeward deck.
Now and then the tiller bucks, our wake
a creamy scar healing as it slips away.
From the cockpit I lean out, look upwards
to a lantern of sun scooped in the sail.
If I duck I see land beneath the boom,
a house, white balcony, a figure watching
– us perhaps: the yachtsman and his crew
squinting at dark trees massed behind the house
like a future whose events do not
include them, their small boat bouncing in spray,
the slap of halyards, the creak of stays.
We could just keep sailing, right off the picture
I shout. My quiet companion smiles and nods.
Already there's a bell. We're at the buoy.
Wordlessly we move, prepare to go about.